GROUP

→ *Video Experience* ←

TONY EVANS
KINGDOM
MARRIAGE

CONNECTING GOD'S PURPOSE
WITH YOUR PLEASURE

TYNDALE HOUSE PUBLISHERS, INC.
CAROL STREAM, ILLINOIS

Contents

Welcome, Kingdom Couples!

Marriage is under attack, according to Dr. Tony Evans. The key to building a relationship that survives and thrives is to embrace God's original purpose for marriage.

Kingdom marriage is a covenantal union between a man and a woman who commit themselves to function in unison under divine authority in order to replicate God's image and expand His rule in the world through their individual calling.

The pursuit of a kingdom marriage will expand your vision of how a marital relationship should function and what it can accomplish. As you work your way through the DVD sessions and this guide, you'll discover Bible-based principles for reigniting the spark in your relationship. You'll also learn what God can do with two people who are fiercely devoted to Him—and to one another.

At the core of each session is a video presentation featuring Dr. Evans, author of *Kingdom Marriage*. Dr. Evans' inspired teaching will give spouses new insights into their relationship as well as their potential.

To make these truths come alive, you'll find these sections in each session:

The Gathering

Read this brief excerpt to focus on the subject at hand. Answer the questions that follow the passage. If you run out of time, finish the section at home.

Show Time!

Use this section as you view and think about the DVD presentation; it includes thought-provoking questions and biblical input.

Transformation Moments

This brief wrap-up will help you find encouragement and ideas for applying the teaching to your own marriage.

Note: The DVD presentations and this guide are intended as general advice only, and are not meant to replace clinical counseling, medical treatment, legal counsel, or pastoral guidance.

Focus on the Family maintains a referral network of Christian counselors. For information, call 1-800-A FAMILY (1-800-232-6459) and ask for the counseling department.

1

FINDING GOD'S PURPOSE FOR YOUR MARRIAGE

The Main Point

When you treat your marriage as a covenant with God, everything else—including love, happiness, satisfaction, and fulfillment—will fall into place.

The Gathering

To find out more about God's purpose for marriage, read the following excerpt from *Kingdom Marriage*. If you have time, answer the questions that appear at the end of the selection. Or you can finish the section at home.

 ### YOUR TRUE PURPOSE

Passion matters and happiness is great, but rather than being the purpose for marriage, they are benefits. Marriage exists to glorify God by expanding

His rule and reach. It uniquely reflects His image like nothing else. When you pursue God's purpose as a couple, then everything else you value in life—such as happiness, love, and satisfaction—will fall into place. . . .

The problem today is that we have transposed the benefit of marriage with the goal, so that when the benefit—happiness—is not working out, we quit and move on, or we resign ourselves to living a life of unhappiness. A large percentage of marriages end in divorce, and many couples who remain together do so out of economic or practical constraints, not love and a shared purpose. Again, kingdom couples share a purpose, not just passion. Emotions change, but the purpose remains and is what can tie two people together until death do they part. . . .

Marriage is not merely a social contract; it is a sacred covenant. It is not simply a means of looking for love, happiness, and fulfillment. Those things are important; in fact, they are critical. But they are not the most important or the most critical. Yet because we have put second things first, as important as second things are, we're having trouble living out either. When God's purpose and principles for marriage are undermined, His image becomes distorted, and our ability to influence others on God's behalf erodes.

Kingdom couples must view marriage through God's kingdom lens. A kingdom marriage is defined as "a covenantal union between a man and a woman who commit themselves to function in unison under divine authority in order to replicate God's image and expand His rule in the world through both their individual and joint callings."[1]

If someone had asked you on your wedding day what the purpose of marriage is, what would you have said? Who or what influenced and shaped your view of marriage—for better or worse? What would happen to your relationship if you focused more on advancing God's kingdom and less on finding your own happiness and fulfillment?

Show Time!

In session 1 of the *Kingdom Marriage Group Video Experience*, Dr. Evans lays out God's purpose for marriage and Satan's plan to thwart that purpose.

After viewing Tony Evans' presentation, "Finding God's Purpose for Your Marriage," use the following questions to help you think through what you saw and heard.

1. Dr. Evans says, "Kingdom marriage is defined as 'a covenantal union between a man and a woman who commit themselves to function in unison under divine authority in order to replicate God's image and expand His rule in the world through both their individual and joint callings.'"

    Which of the following words describe your reaction to this definition of marriage as God intends it to be?

Check the boxes of the ones that apply or write in your own responses.

- ☐ overwhelmed
- ☐ excited
- ☐ unprepared
- ☐ optimistic
- ☐ confident
- ☐ curious
- ☐ desperate
- ☐ doubtful
- ☐ willing
- ☐ uncertain
- ☐ ashamed
- ☐ thankful
- ☐ eager
- ☐ ready
- ☐ other _____
- ☐ other _____
- ☐ other _____

In one sentence, explain the emotion that's hitting you hardest as you begin this study of kingdom marriage.

2. The Bible describes God's purpose for marriage in Genesis
   1:26: "Let Us make man in Our image, according to Our
   likeness; and let them rule over the fish of the sea and over
   the birds of the sky and over the cattle and over all the earth,
   and over every creeping thing that creeps on the earth."

   How would our world be different if all couples took
   their kingdom marriage covenant seriously?

   What would change in your world—in your marriage,
   your home, your circle of influence—if you and your spouse
   committed to a relationship that actively seeks to mirror God
   and expand His rule in the world?

3. Which of the following areas of conflict have caused
   problems in your marriage? Check the boxes of the ones
   that apply or write in your own.

   ☐ finances
   ☐ sexual intimacy

- ☐ parenting style
- ☐ friends
- ☐ family
- ☐ personal habits
- ☐ priorities
- ☐ expectations
- ☐ household responsibilities
- ☐ unresolved issues from the past
- ☐ personality conflicts
- ☐ substance abuse
- ☐ time apart
- ☐ other _____
- ☐ other _____
- ☐ other _____

What role does Satan play in each of those problem areas?

4. In discussing the command not to eat of the tree in the middle of the Garden of Eden, Dr. Evans quotes God as saying, "You have the choice. The choice is between *human*

reasoning (good and evil; you figure it out) or *revelation* (what I reveal)."

Dr. Evans continues, "Most of our marriages have been influenced by the homes we grew up in . . . , the people we know who are as miserable as we are, what the media says about it, or the environment in which we live. All of those influence our perspectives on marriage. Everybody has an idea."

How has your marriage been influenced by human reasoning—specifically . . .

- the homes you and your spouse grew up in?

- unhappily married family members, friends, and acquaintances?

- portrayals of marriage online and in movies, TV shows, books, and magazines?

• the culture you live in?

What specific steps can you take to prevent those influences from overshadowing God's revelation?

5. Think back to Dr. Evans' story about trying to assemble a bicycle without using the instructions. Why do many couples try to assemble their marriage without consulting God's "instruction manual"?

What are some of the dangers of trying to assemble a relationship on your own?

6. Read the following excerpt from *Kingdom Marriage* and reflect on the questions at the end.

 ## The Cosmic Conflict

Satan, a created creature, is no match for the all-powerful Creator. That's no fight. Yet what God did establish was the opportunity for inferior creatures—human beings (Psalm 8:5)—to demonstrate that in this spiritual battle, even we can win when we operate according to God's kingdom rule. We are in an ongoing battle, and Satan has had thousands of years to perfect his punches. He likes to target married couples first, since we ultimately reflect the union of Christ with the church, as well as pass down the image of God to the next generation. As kingdom couples, we have been cast in a cosmic conflict to manifest God's rule in history for the advancement of His kingdom and the reflection of His glory.

God has delegated the managerial responsibility for ruling on earth. We hold that responsibility. Yet keep in mind that He has not turned over *absolute* ownership of the earth to us. By turning over the management to us, He has established a process, within certain boundaries, wherein He respects our decisions even if they go against His own, or even if those decisions are not in the best interest of that which is being managed. As a result, we either experience blessing or the consequences of poor decisions.

. . . Your decisions as a couple regarding both how you relate to each other and how you reflect God to others through your union directly affect the quality of life you experience. The tragedy for most couples is that they have followed suit with Satan, seeking ownership rights, not just management responsibilities. As owners, couples go outside of God's rule and make decisions based on their preferred will or desires. And like Satan, they experience the distance and conflict he did when he was booted from God's presence.

What that means is that you can have a happy marriage or a miserable marriage depending on whether or not you exercise your rule as a reflection of God's image. God isn't going to make you rule according to His rule. He isn't going to force you to have a productive and fulfilling relationship. He established marriage and its purposes, but you have the option of living by those purposes or not.

Frequently the well-being of a marriage is determined by whether the husband and wife are reflecting God's image in their individual roles. Once that mirror shatters or even cracks, the reflection of the relationship breaks with it. Nearly every time there's a family breakdown, it is the result of one or both spouses operating outside the covenantal bonds of marriage. They are modeling a broken mirror. As a result, they experience less of God's favor.

Satan either tries to get us to relinquish our management and hand it over to him by deceiving us into believing that he has authority, or he tries to get us to manage poorly based on our own judgments and distorted worldviews. He often does this through the promotion of conflict in our relationships, or through the enticement of ungodly choices.

When we as couples fail to align ourselves under God's kingdom rule, the battle lines are drawn.[2]

What battle strategies has Satan used in the past to negatively affect your marriage? How did you respond to his attacks? What specific steps can you take—as individuals and as a couple—to reflect God more clearly in your marriage?

Transformation Moments

Read the following passage from the book of Psalms. Answer the questions that follow the passage. If you run out of time, finish this section at home.

The Lord's Glory and Man's Dignity

O Lord, our Lord,
How majestic is Your name in all the earth,

Who have displayed Your splendor above the heavens!
From the mouth of infants and nursing babes You have
    established strength
Because of Your adversaries,
To make the enemy and the revengeful cease.

When I consider Your heavens, the work of Your fingers,
The moon and the stars, which You have ordained;
What is man that You take thought of him,
And the son of man that You care for him?
Yet You have made him a little lower than God,
And You crown him with glory and majesty!
You make him to rule over the works of Your hands;
You have put all things under his feet,
All sheep and oxen,
And also the beasts of the field,
The birds of the heavens and the fish of the sea,
Whatever passes through the paths of the seas.

O LORD, our Lord,
How majestic is Your name in all the earth!

PSALM 8:1–9

The phrase "a little lower than God" also can be translated as "a little lower than the angels." In what ways are humans a little lower than angels? Why does God prefer to use the "lowly" to accomplish His work? How can we use the psalmist's words as inspiration or motivation to pursue a kingdom marriage?

2

❖❖❖❖❖❖

HONORING THE COVENANT OF MARRIAGE

The Main Point
Married couples will enjoy God's blessings and inheritance as long as they stay under the "umbrella" of His marriage covenant.

The Gathering
To find out more about God's protective umbrella, read the following excerpt from *Kingdom Marriage*. If you have time, answer the questions that appear at the end of the selection. Or you can finish the section at home.

 ## UMBRELLA COVERAGE

If and when you operate under God's covenant, you are operating under His covering. Consider this analogy: When it is raining outside, most people will open an umbrella. The umbrella covers them from the rain. The umbrella doesn't stop the rain, but it does stop the rain from reaching them. It doesn't change what is happening around a person, but it does change what happens to him or her.

Living under God's covering may not change the challenges you face in your marriage, but under His covering, those challenges won't affect you—cause you to react, worry, or argue—at the level they normally would if you were out from under His covering. That's why it is so critical for spouses to understand the covenantal design of marriage. The marriage vows are a serious set of vows that bring with them either blessing or cursing, depending upon how those vows are honored or dismissed.

The covering of the covenant is a lot like the armor of God that Paul spoke about in Ephesians 6. The armor is there to protect you, but God will never force you to wear it. He's not going to stick the shield of faith in your hand; you have to pick it up. It's there if you need it, but it's up to you whether you use it rightly. Similarly, if it's raining and you have an umbrella but don't use it, you'll get wet. You have to make the choice.[1]

If someone had explained the covenantal design of marriage to you while you were dating, what impact would it have had on your decision to marry? How do you know when you're under the umbrella of God's covering in your marriage? What is the biggest challenge you face in honoring your marriage covenant with God?

Show Time!

In session 2 of the *Kingdom Marriage Group Video Experience*, Dr. Tony Evans identifies the five ingredients of the marriage covenant.

After viewing Tony Evans' presentation, "Honoring the Covenant of Marriage," use the following questions to help you think through what you saw and heard.

1. Which of the following has Satan used in the past to try to pull you from under the umbrella of God's marriage covenant? Check the boxes of the ones that apply or write in your own.

   ❏ financial problems
   ❏ doubt
   ❏ fear
   ❏ temptation

- ☐ disagreements over parenting styles
- ☐ the negative influence of friends
- ☐ the negative influence of family
- ☐ misplaced priorities
- ☐ unrealistic expectations
- ☐ conflicts over household responsibilities
- ☐ unresolved issues from the past
- ☐ time apart
- ☐ other _____
- ☐ other _____
- ☐ other _____

Which ones were most effective? Explain.

2. In 1 Corinthians 11:3, the apostle Paul lays out God's intended chain of command for the marriage covenant: God—Jesus—man—woman.

   Which part of that hierarchy has been the biggest challenge in your relationship? Explain.

What specific steps can you and your spouse take, individually and together, to better align yourselves under God's covenant umbrella?

3. Think about Dr. Evans' statement that in the marriage covenant, whoever is over you represents you. In what ways does . . .

- Jesus represent the man?

- the man represent the woman?

- parents represent their children?

4. Dr. Evans says, "How we handle the rules [of the marriage covenant] not only determines how we fare, but how our children fare, even to the third and fourth generation. . . . When the parents have broken the rules and not fixed it . . . you see children repeating what the father did, what the mother did. A lot of women are living in rebellion because they saw their mother living in rebellion, or they saw their father abusing their mother, and they wind up becoming abusers too."

What generational consequences—or failures of your own parents or grandparents—have you had to overcome in your own relationship?

What safeguards have you built (or will you build) into your relationship to keep from repeating those mistakes?

5. Think back to Dr. Evans' discussion of David and Goliath. David, who was under God's covenant, wasn't intimidated by the size of his opponent. He recognized that Goliath could be defeated.

   What "giant" are you facing in your marriage?

   Why does it seem like such an intimidating opponent?

   What would happen to that giant if you and your spouse attacked it together, under the protection of God's covenant?

6. Read the following excerpt from *Kingdom Marriage* and reflect on the questions at the end.

It Takes Three

As I've said before, marriage is a sacred covenant, not just a social contract. It consists of more than a relationship arranged for the purpose of procreation or even companionship. Marriage provides a unique covenantal environment in which you have an even greater opportunity to live out your destiny both individually and as a couple.

The book of Ecclesiastes is filled with powerful wisdom and insightful truths, such as this principle: "A cord of three strands is not quickly torn apart" (4:12). This is an important key to a successful marriage. When two people enter into a covenant, they enter into it along with a third person, God. Just as the Trinity is made up of three persons who are one—God the Father, God the Son, and God the Holy Spirit—marriage is an earthly replica of this divine Trinity—the husband, the wife, and God.

You cannot leave God at the altar and expect to have a thriving marriage. God must join you in your home. When He does, and when you align yourself within the parameters of love, respect, commitment, and compassion He has established, He can do marvels with your marriage. You cannot do it alone. You cannot even do it as husband and wife. God is the cord that not only keeps you together but also keeps you strong and able to do all He has designed for you to do and enjoy.

God's power is best freed to flow when you recognize and respect the marital covenant as a covenant, not merely as a convenient companionship you entered into. When Christ arose from the dead, He gave humankind access to the power of His resurrection (Romans 6:4; Philippians 3:10) and the presence of the Holy Spirit (John 14:16–18). That power can enable you and your mate to live together, love each other, trust each other, and share life with each other until death parts you.

God made marriage, and because He did, He knows just what you need to make yours not only survive but also thrive. Commit yourselves to Him by functioning within the parameters of His divinely orchestrated covenant of marriage. As you do, He will strengthen your marriage into something that He can use not only to glorify Himself but to bring you and your spouse fulfillment, purpose, and pleasure.[2]

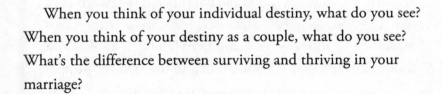

When you think of your individual destiny, what do you see? When you think of your destiny as a couple, what do you see? What's the difference between surviving and thriving in your marriage?

Transformation Moments

Read the following passage from the book of Malachi. Answer the questions that follow the passage. If you run out of time, finish this section at home.

 A COVENANT TO KEEP

"Do we not all have one father? Has not one God created us? Why do we deal treacherously each against his brother so as to profane the covenant of our fathers? Judah has dealt treacherously, and an abomination has been committed in Israel and in Jerusalem; for Judah has profaned the sanctuary of the LORD which He loves and has married the daughter of a foreign god. As for the man who does this, may the LORD cut off from the tents of Jacob everyone who awakes and answers, or who presents an offering to the LORD of hosts.

"This is another thing you do: you cover the altar of the LORD with tears, with weeping and with groaning, because He no longer regards the offering or accepts it with favor from your hand. Yet you say, 'For what reason?' Because the LORD has been a witness between you and the wife of your youth, against whom you have dealt treacherously, though she is your companion and your wife by covenant. But not one has done so who has a remnant of the Spirit. And what did that one do while he was seeking a godly offspring? Take heed then to your spirit, and let no one deal treacherously against the wife of your youth. For I hate divorce," says the LORD, the God of Israel, "and him who covers his garment with wrong," says the LORD of hosts. "So take heed to your spirit, that you do not deal treacherously."

You have wearied the LORD with your words. Yet you say, "How have we wearied Him?" In that you say, "Everyone who does evil is good in the sight of the LORD, and He delights in them," or, "Where is the God of justice?"

MALACHI 2:10–17

What are some examples of dealing "treacherously" with your spouse? Why don't people make a bigger deal of God's declaration, "I hate divorce"? What happens in a marriage when the option of divorce is taken off the table?

3

EMBRACING THE UNITY OF MARRIAGE

The Main Point

Marital unity involves a husband and wife combining their unique talents and gifts with a oneness of purpose to advance God's kingdom.

The Gathering

To find out more about how to become one with your spouse, read the following excerpt from *Kingdom Marriage*. If you have time, answer the questions that appear at the end of the selection. Or you can finish the section at home.

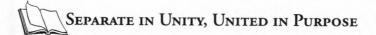

SEPARATE IN UNITY, UNITED IN PURPOSE

Unfortunately, some couples enter into marriage with a distorted view of unity, and their unrealistic expectations contribute to future disappointments. I see this at times when I perform wedding ceremonies. Often a portion of the ceremony includes two candles, which were lit prior to the ceremony and are then joined together to light an entirely new candle, thus symbolizing the unity of marriage. But it's a mistake when the bride and groom then blow out their individual candles.

I say this is a mistake because unless there is an intentional protection and respect for each other's unique identities, purposes, talents, skills, and callings, a couple is prone to fall prey to a marriage that consumes them rather than compels them both to greatness. When I meet with couples whose weddings I'm going to perform, I suggest that they don't blow out their individual candles after lighting a new, unified candle. Imagine attending a symphony where each musical instrument was a flute. It wouldn't be long before you would leave that symphony altogether. Rather, you hear beautiful music at a symphony because each unique instrument plays in harmony. That's what biblical unity in marriage ought to represent: the distinct lives of two individuals experiencing God's purpose for each of them in harmony with the other.

The Father didn't become the Son in order to be unified with Christ in the Trinity. The Holy Spirit didn't become the Father either. The reason the Trinity works so well in carrying out its various functions in our lives is because each member of the Trinity honors and respects the other and doesn't seek to become the other.

What I'm saying may seem out of place in a chapter specifically dedicated to oneness in marriage, but unless we understand and live out *true* unity in our marriages, we run the risk of cannibalizing each other not long after we say "I do." The healthiest marriages I've seen are those in which both parties maintain separate identities and purposes as they unite under the shared purpose of fulfilling the dominion rule of God in and through their partnership.[1]

Why do some spouses believe they need to "blow out their individual candles" when they get married? What unique talents, gifts, and perspectives did your spouse bring to your marriage? How can you help your spouse maintain his or her separate identity?

Show Time!

In session 3 of the *Kingdom Marriage Group Video Experience*, Dr. Tony Evans underscores the importance of working toward oneness in marriage.

After viewing Tony Evans' presentation, "Embracing the Unity of Marriage," use the following questions to help you think through what you saw and heard.

1. Dr. Evans uses the analogy of a football team to describe the kind of unity God desires in married couples. What are some of the positions or roles you play on your "marriage team"? Check the boxes of the ones that apply or write in your own responses.

   ❐ protector
   ❐ intimacy expert
   ❐ sounding board
   ❐ provider
   ❐ advisor
   ❐ leader
   ❐ spiritual need–meeter
   ❐ point person
   ❐ servant
   ❐ decision maker
   ❐ other _____
   ❐ other _____
   ❐ other _____

   Which of those roles come naturally to you?

Which ones are most challenging for you?

2. "This thing of fighting and fussing and cussing and dividing is theological and spiritual. It's not just relational and personal." With these words from Dr. Evans in mind, what changes will you make in the way you approach conflict with your spouse?

How can you "preserve the unity of the Spirit," as the apostle Paul urges in Ephesians 4, even in the midst of a disagreement with your spouse?

3. Dr. Evans points out that you're *supposed* to be different from your mate. In what ways do the differences between you and your spouse make life interesting . . .

- in the kitchen?

- in your social life?

- in your approach to finances?

- in your parenting styles?

- in your spiritual life?

- in the way you deal with conflict?

4. If Satan were to try to disconnect your relationship with the Lord God, what would be his most likely plan of attack?

Why is that area of your life vulnerable?

5. What "relationship fixes" have you tried in the past? Check the boxes of the ones that apply or write in your own responses.

- ❑ talking to your pastor
- ❑ talking to a marriage counselor
- ❑ living apart
- ❑ having a baby

- ☐ going to church
- ☐ taking a vacation (perhaps a cruise)
- ☐ moving to a new area
- ☐ reading marriage books and articles
- ☐ changing jobs
- ☐ other _____
- ☐ other _____
- ☐ other _____

What were the results?

6. Read the following excerpt from *Kingdom Marriage* and reflect on the questions at the end.

 ## THE EMULSIFIER

One of the challenges of making mayonnaise is getting the oil and vinegar to come together. Oil and liquids do not mix, but they are necessary ingredients in mayonnaise. So what the makers of mayonnaise do is introduce an emulsifier into the ingredients.

An emulsifier helps ingredients that are at odds with each other to get along, to blend. So a necessary ingredient in mayonnaise is the emulsifier: eggs. The eggs say, "I want you, oil, over here to hang out with me, and I want you, vinegar, to hang out with me too." When eggs get mixed in with the vinegar and oil, the vinegar and oil will now hang out with each other. Not because vinegar and oil like each other but because both of them can agree on eggs, and as a result, something greater than the individual parts is created—mayonnaise.

The Holy Spirit is the emulsifier in any marriage. When there is ongoing conflict between Christian husbands and wives, one or both parties have ignored the emulsifying work of the Holy Spirit. As a result, they can no longer point to the shared work of the Spirit in their lives, in spite of any differences of taste or opinion that might exist.

Paul emphasized this truth by telling the Ephesian Christians that the relational oneness that characterizes unity is "preserved," not created. They are to "preserve the unity of the Spirit in the bond of peace" (Ephesians 4:3). When it comes to marriage, God is not inviting us to create anything. He's inviting us to preserve what He's already created. We have entered into a relationship with Him through His Spirit, and as a result, He is already present and at work in the midst of our marriages.

Paul's challenge to "preserve the unity of the Spirit" is complemented by his notice that this unity of the Spirit exists "in the bond of peace" (4:3). Paul's concept of peace here is much broader than our modern definition of an absence of conflict or a feeling of harmony. Paul was likely pointing to the Hebrew concept of *shalom*, defined as "wholeness, health, and well-being." Shalom is more than just peace between two parties; it indicates the overall health and balance of an organism. So when we preserve the unity of the Spirit, the outcome is a healthy, balanced marriage in which to fully live out and experience abundant life.

A healthy marriage is a unified marriage, where the presence and work of God's Spirit transcends our individual differences. Satan seeks to disrupt the unity in our marriages in order to bring about disorder, which ultimately leads to chaos.[2]

What makes two people who are "oil" and "liquid" believe they can get together in the first place? What specifically has the Holy Spirit done to make you and your spouse more compatible? What would your marriage be like without the emulsifying work of the Holy Spirit?

Transformation Moments

Read the following passage from the book of 1 Corinthians. Answer the questions that follow the passage. If you run out of time, finish this section at home.

SEXUAL FASTING

Now concerning the things about which you wrote, it is good for a man not to touch a woman. But because of immoralities, each man is to have his own wife, and each woman is to have her own husband. The husband must fulfill his duty to his wife, and likewise also the wife to her husband. The wife does not have authority over her own body, but the husband does; and likewise also the husband does not have authority over his own body, but the wife does. Stop depriving one another, except by agreement for a time, so that you may devote yourselves to prayer, and come together again so that Satan will not tempt you because of your lack of self-control. But this I say by way of concession, not of command. Yet I wish that all men were even as I myself am. However, each man has his own gift from God, one in this manner, and another in that.

I CORINTHIANS 7:1−7

What type of situation might call for a sexual fast? In a best-case scenario, what might a sexual fast accomplish? What might happen if God's guidelines for a sexual fast aren't followed?

4

LOVE YOUR WIFE

The Main Point
A husband's role in marriage is to love his wife, compassionately and righteously pursuing her well-being.

The Gathering
To find out more about God's role for husbands, read the following excerpt from *Kingdom Marriage*. If you have time, answer the questions that appear at the end of the selection. Or you can finish the section at home.

EVERYDAY SACRIFICES

We men are great at saying the right things. We can sound very impressive to our wives when we want to, talking about how we will be there for them and protect them and even die for them if necessary.

But we're not crazy. We know that the chances of this happening are very remote. I personally can't think of one man I know who has died or even been injured defending his wife from a crazed intruder, and chances are you can't either. That's not going to happen to most of us, or to anyone we know. So we're pretty safe declaring that we would make the ultimate sacrifice for our wives.

But for most of us, it's another story when it comes to the everyday sacrifices of married life—surrendering or yielding our desires, opinions, preferences, and plans for our wives. When God calls husbands to give themselves up for their wives, He is not simply talking about being willing to die. Sacrificing for our wives and loving them involves being willing to nail our desires and agendas to the cross to meet their needs.

This brings us to the area where we fail so often as husbands: selfishness. It's difficult for most men to give up our wants for our wives. Yet a husband should let his love be visible and tangible so that his wife can experience how much he values her.[1]

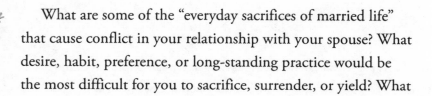

What are some of the "everyday sacrifices of married life" that cause conflict in your relationship with your spouse? What desire, habit, preference, or long-standing practice would be the most difficult for you to sacrifice, surrender, or yield? What would be the impact—on your spouse and on yourself—if you were to give it up?

Show Time!
In session 4 of the *Kingdom Marriage Group Video Experience*, Dr. Tony Evans reveals how a husband can transform his marriage by deciding to love his wife.

After viewing Tony Evans' presentation, "Love Your Wife," use the following questions to help you think through what you saw and heard.

1. Think back to Dr. Evans' story about the garage door that wouldn't open because the sensors weren't aligned. Using his experience as an analogy of marriage, how might a couple tell if their marriage is "stuck"?

What kind of problems make it too heavy to lift?

What buttons do couples push in an effort to get their relationship unstuck?

Give an example of a small adjustment that might make a big difference.

2. In Ephesians 5:33, the apostle Paul offers this instruction to husbands: "Each individual among you also is to love his own wife even as himself." With those words in mind, take the following true-false quiz. After each question, give a short explanation of your answer.

True or false? Love is something you fall into and out of.

True or false? Love trumps emotion.

True or false? Love is a decision.

3. Which of the following factors make it difficult for you to love your spouse as the Bible commands? Check the boxes of the ones that apply or write in your own responses.

- ❏ your own family history
- ❏ boredom with the relationship
- ❏ your feelings for another person
- ❏ your spouse's history
- ❏ your spouse's attitude toward you
- ❏ unresolved conflict
- ❏ differing priorities
- ❏ lack of common interests
- ❏ physical changes in your spouse
- ❏ physical changes in you

☐ other _____

☐ other _____

☐ other _____

What changes can you make—to your relationship, your daily routine, and yourself—to overcome each of these difficulties?

4. Describe your spouse in a way that highlights his or her unique gifts, abilities, and calling. (Be generous in your praise.)

In a given week, how much time do you spend making your spouse feel genuinely appreciated, admired, and loved?

What would happen if you doubled that amount of time this week?

5. In response to men who claim they married the "wrong" woman, Dr. Evans makes the point that if you treat the wrong woman like the *right* woman, she may become the right woman.

   With those words in mind, what *specific* instructions would you give to a friend who confided in you that he believes his marriage is a mistake?

6. Read the following excerpt from *Kingdom Marriage* and reflect on the questions at the end.

KNOWING, HONORING, AND PRAYING WITH YOUR WIFE

The other three roles husbands are to fulfill in marriage are knowing their wives, honoring them, and praying with them. To live with your wife means to dwell in close harmony with her, making your home a place of intimacy and mutual support. Many husbands approach their family life with the attitude that the home and the responsibilities that go with it are primarily the wife's job. However, if the husband is to live with his wife "in an understanding way" (1 Peter 3:7), he must see the home as a primary place to exercise Christ's mandate of sacrificial, self-giving love. The husband must be committed to the home as a place of vocation and calling in addition to his workplace. Whenever the things you do for your wife outside of your home (such as your career) diminish your presence with her to a large degree, then you aren't living with her in the way 1 Peter 3:7 describes.

To live with your wife "in an understanding way" also means that the husband is responsible for intimately knowing his wife. This means that he must be committed to taking the time to come to know her and making necessary adjustments in his schedule to open up space for that.

Another role of the husband is to "honor" his wife "as a fellow heir of the grace of life" (verse 7). To grant honor to your wife is to place her in a position of significance and treat her as someone unique. Whether through kind words, special gifts, or notes telling her how much you love her, you have a responsibility to let your wife know that she is special.

A true commitment to honor your wife means more than just honoring her on special days (birthdays, anniversaries, Valentine's Day); it means consistently communicating to her the value you place on your relationship. Just as God's lovingkindnesses are new every morning (Lamentations 3:22–23), so we as kingdom leaders should show that same consistency to our wives.

The husband's mandate to honor his wife is rooted in the recognition that she is "a fellow heir of the grace of life." Though the wife is called to submit to her husband, this is a relationship of function, not a statement of her inequality as a person. Like the man, she's created in the image of God and worthy of honor as the man's spiritual equal in the eyes of God. Do you treat and view your wife as an equal? One way to know if you do is whether you seek her counsel when you're faced with a decision. Another way is if you seek her company when you have free time or leisure time.

Finally, a husband's role is to pray with his wife. At the root of the command for the husband to live with his wife in an understanding way (to know her) and honor her is this warning: "so that your prayers will not be hindered" (1 Peter 3:7). Since the wife is a "fellow heir of the grace of life," God will not do anything for the husband unless the wife is included. God views the marriage covenant as entering into a "one flesh" relationship; thus, the wife is now included in any interaction God has with the husband. The husband, then, must be committed to praying with his wife so that together they can reap the spiritual benefits of God's kingdom plan.[2]

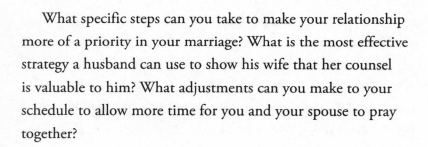

What specific steps can you take to make your relationship more of a priority in your marriage? What is the most effective strategy a husband can use to show his wife that her counsel is valuable to him? What adjustments can you make to your schedule to allow more time for you and your spouse to pray together?

Transformation Moments

Read the following passage from the book of Ephesians. Answer the questions that follow the passage. If you run out of time, finish this section at home.

As Christ Loved the Church

Husbands, love your wives, just as Christ also loved the church and gave Himself up for her, so that He might sanctify her, having cleansed her by the washing of water with the word, that He might present to Himself the church in all her glory, having no spot or wrinkle or any such thing; but that she would be holy and blameless. So husbands ought also to love their own wives as their own bodies. He who loves his own wife loves himself; for no one ever hated his own flesh, but nourishes and cherishes it, just as Christ also does the church, because we are members of His body. For this reason a man shall leave his father and mother and shall be joined to his wife, and the two shall become one flesh. This mystery is great; but I am speaking with reference to Christ and the church. Nevertheless, each individual among you also is to love his own wife even as himself, and the wife must see to it that she respects her husband.

EPHESIANS 5:25–33

How would you describe Christ's love for the church? How does it feel to be on the receiving end of His love? How can you, in turn, show the same kind of love to your spouse?

5

❖❖❖❖❖❖

RESPECT YOUR HUSBAND

The Main Point

A wife's role in marriage is to respect her husband, to esteem him greatly, and to give proper recognition to his position.

The Gathering

To find out more about God's role for wives, read the following excerpt from *Kingdom Marriage*. If you have time, answer the questions that appear at the end of the selection. Or you can finish the section at home.

 ## THE HIGH CALLING OF A WIFE

When God created Eve for Adam (the woman to connect with the man), He did so for a specific purpose, and that purpose is much more significant than most of us ever realize.

Much of the confusion we experience in our marriages today comes from an inaccurate view of this purpose. When we read that God said it wasn't good for Adam to be alone, we assume that Eve came along to provide companionship. But if God had created Eve for companionship, then Adam probably would have said that he didn't like being alone. But it was God who said that, not Adam. That's an important point we often skip over, so let that sink in. Also, the Hebrew words used to describe the woman as a "helper" don't refer to someone who relieves loneliness. It refers to someone who provides viable and visible help.

There is only one reason God would say, "I will make him a helper suitable for him" (Genesis 2:18), and it's that Adam obviously needed help.

I'm not negating the importance of companionship, friendship, and relationship in marriage. But based on the historical law of first mention with regard to marriage in the Bible, companionship for Adam wasn't God's primary concern when He made the woman. It was about empowering Adam to exercise rule in God's name at an even greater level than he could alone. . . .

Wives, if you view your role as only cooking food, cleaning the house, wiping noses, driving kids to soccer or dance practice, and so on, you have missed your role. Chores are necessary and food is important, but depending on where you are in this stage of your life, you could hire someone for those tasks, or your husband could share the load. As a wife, you have a high calling to discover with your spouse how God wants the two of you to best use your skills, talents, time, and treasure to advance His kingdom on this earth.[1]

How would you respond to someone who believes that a wife's primary role is companionship? What can you and your spouse accomplish together that you can't accomplish individually? What's the first step in discovering God's high calling for you and your spouse?

Show Time!

In session 5 of the *Kingdom Marriage Group Video Experience*, Dr. Tony Evans reveals how a wife can transform her marriage by submitting to her husband's legitimate authority.

After viewing Tony Evans' presentation, "Respect Your Husband," use the following questions to help you think through what you saw and heard.

1. Is it possible for a wife to love her husband without respecting him? Explain.

Is it possible for a wife to respect her husband without loving him? Explain.

2. In Ephesians 5:22, the apostle Paul says, "Wives, be subject to your own husbands, as to the Lord." The words "be subject" are also translated as "submit." Dr. Evans refers to it as "the s-word." Why is submission such a controversial subject in our culture?

Why are the words "as to the Lord" so important to understanding the kind of submission Paul is talking about?

Why is Jesus' model of submission to His heavenly Father helpful in understanding a wife's submission to her husband?

3. Describe the God-given role of a wife in terms of the Hebrew phrase Dr. Evans celebrates—*ezer kenegdo*, which is translated "helper suitable for him" in Genesis 2:18.

What does it mean to you that the term *ezer kenegdo* is used most often to describe the kind of help God Himself offers?

4. "Therefore the woman ought to have a symbol of authority on her head, because of the angels" (1 Corinthians 11:10). In explaining this difficult passage, Dr. Evans points out that angels are messengers. They assist in carrying our requests to God and delivering His responses to us. Why is it so important for a woman to be under her proper authority, especially where the work of angels is concerned?

What can a wife who is under the proper authority in marriage accomplish that her husband, if he *isn't* under proper authority, can't?

5. Dr. Evans closes the session by using the story of "Beauty and the Beast" to describe what happens when a wife devotes herself to her role as *ezer kenegdo*. In your experience, what specific things can a woman do to "humanize" her husband?

In your experience, what changes do people notice in a man who's been "humanized"—that is, respected and loved—by his wife?

6. Read the following excerpt from *Kingdom Marriage* and
   reflect on the questions at the end.

SATAN'S GREAT REVERSAL

When Satan tempted Eve in the Garden of Eden, he wanted to turn
the order in marriage on its head. Satan is happy when wives assume
the leadership role over their husbands. But just as God held Adam
responsible for failing to lead Eve well in the garden, He will hold men
accountable for abdicating their role in the family. And just as Eve was at
fault for ignoring Adam's leadership as he stood with her in the presence
of the serpent, God will hold wives accountable for disregarding their
husbands' legitimate headship.

After Adam and Eve fell to Satan's temptation, a curse fell on all of
creation. God told Eve that as a result of her disobedience, she and all of
her female descendants would want to take leadership in the family, but
their husbands would desire to dominate them (Genesis 3:16). Thank-
fully, Christ has reversed the curse and gives wives and husbands the grace
to live in harmony according to God's original design.

It's pretty easy for a wife to submit to her husband if he loves the Lord
and walks in obedience to Him. But what if he doesn't? Does God still
require submission if a husband isn't living as a Christian? Here's a better
question: Can God still lead a family when the husband isn't walking with

Him? Yes. God is sovereign, and wives can surrender completely to Him, trusting that He will not only work through a disobedient husband, but He can transform that husband's heart through the honor and respect his wife shows him.

When a wife is willing to surrender herself *first* to the Lord, only then will she be able to properly submit to her husband. And when God sees that a wife trusts in Him enough to honor her husband's role, He will work in amazing and even miraculous ways to bless and guide her family, just as He did for Sarah (1 Peter 3:6).[2]

What causes men to abdicate their role in the family? What causes women to disregard their husbands' legitimate headship? What specific steps can you and your spouse take to make sure you maintain your God-given roles in marriage?

Transformation Moments

Read the following passage from the book of Proverbs. Answer the questions that follow the passage. If you run out of time, finish this section at home.

An Excellent Wife

An excellent wife, who can find?
For her worth is far above jewels.
The heart of her husband trusts in her,
And he will have no lack of gain.
She does him good and not evil
All the days of her life.
She looks for wool and flax
And works with her hands in delight.
She is like merchant ships;
She brings her food from afar.
She rises also while it is still night
And gives food to her household
And portions to her maidens.
She considers a field and buys it;
From her earnings she plants a vineyard.
She girds herself with strength
And makes her arms strong.
She senses that her gain is good;
Her lamp does not go out at night.

She stretches out her hands to the distaff,

And her hands grasp the spindle.

She extends her hand to the poor,

And she stretches out her hands to the needy.

She is not afraid of the snow for her household,

For all her household are clothed with scarlet.

She makes coverings for herself;

Her clothing is fine linen and purple.

Her husband is known in the gates,

When he sits among the elders of the land.

She makes linen garments and sells them,

And supplies belts to the tradesmen.

Strength and dignity are her clothing,

And she smiles at the future.

She opens her mouth in wisdom,

And the teaching of kindness is on her tongue.

She looks well to the ways of her household,

And does not eat the bread of idleness.

Her children rise up and bless her;

Her husband also, and he praises her, saying:

"Many daughters have done nobly,

But you excel them all."

Charm is deceitful and beauty is vain,

But a woman who fears the LORD, she shall be praised.

Give her the product of her hands,
And let her works praise her in the gates.

PROVERBS 31:10–31

How might a wife today make her husband "known in the gates"? What are modern-day equivalents to activities such as "she brings her food from afar" and "she considers a field and buys it"? What specific—and personal—lines would you add to this description of an excellent wife? (In other words, husbands, describe ways in which your wife excels.) In addition to sharing your revised version of Proverbs 31, what are some creative ways you can show appreciation and encouragement to your spouse?

REKINDLING YOUR FIRST LOVE

The Main Point

Repositioning the priority of your relationship is the key to rekindling your first love and getting back what you may have lost as a couple.

The Gathering

To find out more about rekindling your first love, read the following excerpt from *Kingdom Marriage*. If you have time, answer the questions that appear at the end of the selection. Or you can finish the section at home.

 ## You Have Left Your First Love

A church had been birthed in Ephesus through the work and ministry of the apostle Paul, and in the beginning, the people in the church were on fire for God (Acts 19). They had brought out their trinkets, magic books, and anything associated with their old way of life and literally set it all ablaze out of devotion to God. Their relationship with the Lord was one of passion, zeal, and connection.

Many relationships are like this when couples first get married. Personal sacrifice doesn't feel like sacrifice. Devotion comes naturally. Yet over time, as we will see in Revelation, that passion somehow morphs into performance as something in the relationship fizzles. . . .

Let's look at how this unfolds for the church of Ephesus, where what started out as a strong commendation for doing great things ended up revealing an empty heart beneath it all: "I know your deeds and your toil and perseverance, and that you cannot tolerate evil men, and you put to the test those who call themselves apostles, and they are not, and you found them to be false; and you have perseverance and have endured for My name's sake, and have not grown weary" (Revelation 2:2–3).

To set the stage, the church of Ephesus had developed into a serving church. What began with a passionate fire for the Lord had produced what most would consider great things. The Ephesian believers were spiritual bumblebees. Everyone was in a ministry, engaged in activity, and doing something to promote good while keeping out evil. . . .

If we were to put this passage in the context of marriage, these are husbands and wives who check items off their to-do lists. They read the Word, play with the kids, and perform the actions that ought to make for a strong home. They don't give in to laziness or selfishness but rather seek to serve. . . .

However, there is a "but." After all of the accolades and praise for a job well done, God follows His message to the church with a small conjunction that had a large meaning: "*But* I have this against you, that you have left your first love" (Revelation 2:4). In other words, "Yes, church at Ephesus, you have done a lot of great stuff. Yes, you are the recipient of many compliments. *But* I have one major criticism that cancels out the rest: You have left your first love. A lot of things may be going right, but this one wrong thing is majorly wrong."[1]

How does passion morph into performance over time? Why did God call out the Ephesians when they were still doing good things in His name and for His kingdom? Why is first love so important to God?

Show Time!
In session 6 of the *Kingdom Marriage Group Video Experience*, Dr. Tony Evans identifies the steps a couple must take to reignite their passion and rediscover what brought them together in the first place.

After viewing Tony Evans' presentation, "Rekindling Your First Love," use the following questions to help you think through what you saw and heard.

1. Describe the difference between love and first love.

    How can you love someone, but feel no passion for him or her?

    Why would two people who still love each other get divorced?

2. When Jesus visited the home of His friends Mary and Martha, Martha worked hard to do all the things a good

hostess does while Mary sat at Jesus' feet and hung on His every word. What does Dr. Evans mean when he says Mary chose "relationship over program"?

What Martha did wasn't necessarily wrong, though. She was providing an important service, doing what she thought needed to be done. Likewise, many couples who lose sight of their first love aren't necessarily doing *wrong* things. How do you strike a proper balance between programs and relationship in your marriage?

3. Dr. Evans tells the story of almost missing his flight at the Atlanta airport because he was so focused on getting some fried chicken. Why do couples sometimes lose sight of their true purpose—that is, in Dr. Evans' words, the reason they're "at the airport"?

What are some specific things that, like the fried chicken in the story, can distract people—and especially couples—from their true purpose?

What's the best strategy for guarding against potential distractions in your relationship?

4. According to Dr. Evans, the first step in reigniting the fire in your relationship is remembering the early days with your spouse. When you go back to the time before you had kids or a mortgage or anything else together, what do you see?

What was different for you back then?

How do you feel when you recall those days?

5. The second step is to repent, or reverse your course. Using Dr. Evans' analogy of trying to change direction while driving on a major highway, what would taking the "Confession Off-Ramp" mean for you? What do you need to confess?

What does the "Grace Overpass" look like to you? In what specific ways has God extended grace to you? In what specific ways can you extend grace to your spouse?

How will you access the "Restoration On-Ramp"? What specific steps can you and your spouse take to make sure you're headed in the right direction?

6. Read the following excerpt from *Kingdom Marriage* and reflect on the questions at the end.

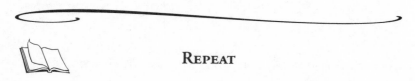

REPEAT

One of the ways to rekindle your relationship is to ask yourself, "Would I have said that or acted this way when we were dating?" If the answer is no, then why would you do it now? Honor your spouse with the same attentiveness and love you showed at the start, and you'll experience a renewal in your relationship.

God has taken us from step 1, which is to remember, to step 2, which is to repent. The last step in returning to our first love is to repeat. God tells us to "do the deeds you did at first" (Revelation 2:5).

Most couples don't date much after they get married. Demands and schedules start to weigh down the relationship, which makes it more and more difficult to date. The modern form of dating is nothing like what happened in Bible times. These days, in America and many other Western countries, people date to get to know someone so they can decide whether they will marry one day. But that's not what we discover in Scripture. In biblical culture, we don't find dating to marry but rather marrying to date. It's the opposite.

A lot of the marriages in biblical times were arranged. The parents often decided whom their children would marry. One reason was that marriage was supposed to be the foundation from which a couple built the relationship, not that which killed it.

As you seek to rekindle the love in your marriage, do the things you used to do when you dated. Repeat those things you did when you were relationship-driven, not program-driven. Repeat special words, kind gestures, dressing up, and remembering the other person's favorite food. Repeat seeking out things to do that you both will enjoy, carving out time when there is none to be had, trying to look your best. Repeat listening when you've heard that story several times before. Or laughing when the joke really isn't that funny. Repeat noticing what it is about your spouse that sets him or her apart from the rest, and then point it out. Repeat these things and more, and you'll rekindle your first love.

Relationships are powerful. The marriage relationship is one of the most intimate, rewarding experiences in life—if you treat it with the honor, attention, and love it deserves. Nourish each other as you first did. Guard yourselves from the "program" of marriage. Make every attempt to remember, repent, and repeat to rekindle that which caused you to marry in the first place.[2]

In what specific ways have you and your spouse changed since you first started dating? What part of your courtship or dating life would you most like to rekindle? Name three things you and your spouse can do this week to begin rekindling your first love.

Transformation Moments

Read the following passage from the book of John. Answer the questions that follow the passage. If you run out of time, finish this section at home.

MIRACLE AT CANA

On the third day there was a wedding in Cana of Galilee, and the mother of Jesus was there; and both Jesus and His disciples were invited to the wedding. When the wine ran out, the mother of Jesus said to Him, "They have no wine." And Jesus said to her, "Woman, what does that have to do with us? My hour has not yet come." His mother said to the servants, "Whatever He says to you, do it." Now there were six stone waterpots set there for the Jewish custom of purification, containing twenty or thirty gallons each. Jesus said to them, "Fill the waterpots with water." So they filled them up to the brim. And He said to them, "Draw some out now and take it to the headwaiter." So they took it to him. When the headwaiter tasted the water which had become wine, and did not know where it came from (but the servants who had drawn the water knew), the headwaiter called the bridegroom, and said to him, "Every man serves the good wine first, and when the people have drunk freely, then he serves the poorer wine; but you have kept the good wine until now." This beginning of His signs Jesus did in Cana of Galilee, and manifested His glory, and His disciples believed in Him.

JOHN 2:1–11

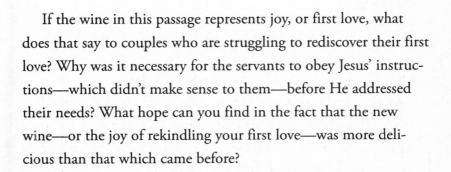

If the wine in this passage represents joy, or first love, what does that say to couples who are struggling to rediscover their first love? Why was it necessary for the servants to obey Jesus' instructions—which didn't make sense to them—before He addressed their needs? What hope can you find in the fact that the new wine—or the joy of rekindling your first love—was more delicious than that which came before?

Notes

SESSION 1: FINDING GOD'S PURPOSE FOR YOUR MARRIAGE
1. Tony Evans, *Kingdom Marriage* (Carol Stream, IL: Focus on the Family/Tyndale House Publishers, 2016), 3–5.
2. Ibid., 14–15.

SESSION 2: HONORING THE COVENANT OF MARRIAGE
1. Tony Evans, *Kingdom Marriage* (Carol Stream, IL: Focus on the Family/Tyndale House Publishers, 2016), 41–42.
2. Ibid., 46–47.

SESSION 3: EMBRACING THE UNITY OF MARRIAGE
1. Tony Evans, *Kingdom Marriage* (Carol Stream, IL: Focus on the Family/Tyndale House Publishers, 2016), 53–54.
2. Ibid., 55–56.

SESSION 4: LOVE YOUR WIFE
1. Tony Evans, *Kingdom Marriage* (Carol Stream, IL: Focus on the Family/Tyndale House Publishers, 2016), 68–69.
2. Ibid., 70–71.

SESSION 5: RESPECT YOUR HUSBAND
1. Tony Evans, *Kingdom Marriage* (Carol Stream, IL: Focus on the Family/Tyndale House Publishers, 2016), 73–74.
2. Ibid., 78–79.

SESSION 6: REKINDLING YOUR FIRST LOVE
1. Tony Evans, *Kingdom Marriage* (Carol Stream, IL: Focus on the Family/Tyndale House Publishers, 2016), 156–158.
2. Ibid., 163–164.

About Dr. Tony Evans

DR. TONY EVANS is the founder and president of The Urban
Alternative, a national ministry dedicated to restoring hope in
personal lives, families, churches, and communities. Dr. Evans
also serves as senior pastor of Oak Cliff Bible Fellowship in
Dallas. He is a best-selling author of numerous books, and his
radio program, *The Alternative with Dr. Tony Evans*, is heard daily
on more than 500 radio stations. Dr. Evans is also the chaplain
for the Dallas Mavericks and former chaplain for the Dallas
Cowboys. For more information, visit TonyEvans.org.

Kingdom Marriage Book and *Kingdom Marriage Group Video Experience* $10 Rebate

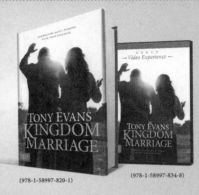

(978-1-58997-820-1)   (978-1-58997-834-8)

GET A $10 REBATE

when you purchase both the *Kingdom Marriage Group Video Experience* and *Kingdom Marriage* hardcover book. Both titles must be purchased at a retail store to qualify. Simply return the completed rebate form (original or photocopy), the original dated store receipt(s) for both products, and the UPC bar code from both packages (original or photocopy) to: Kingdom Marriage Rebate, Attn. Customer Service, 351 Executive Dr., Carol Stream, IL 60188.

NAME _____

ADDRESS _____

CITY _____ STATE _____ ZIP _____

E-MAIL ADDRESS _____

STORE WHERE PURCHASED _____

SIGNATURE _____

THE KINGDOM SERIES FROM DR. TONY EVANS

MORE RESOURCES TO GROW YOUR FAITH AND FURTHER GOD'S KINGDOM!

KINGDOM MAN
978-1-58997-685-6

KINGDOM MAN
DEVOTIONAL
978-1-62405-121-0

KINGDOM WOMAN
978-1-58997-743-3

KINGDOM WOMAN
DEVOTIONAL
978-1-62405-122-7

KINGDOM WOMAN
VIDEO STUDY
978-1-62405-209-5

RAISING KINGDOM KIDS
978-1-58997-784-6

RAISING KINGDOM KIDS
DEVOTIONAL
978-1-62405-409-9

RAISING KINGDOM KIDS
VIDEO STUDY
978-1-62405-407-5

Meet the rest of the family

Expert advice on parenting and marriage . . .
spiritual growth . . . powerful personal stories . . .

Focus on the Family's collection of inspiring, practical resources can help your family grow closer to God—and each other—than ever before. Whichever format you need—video, audio, book, or e-book—we have something for you. Discover how to help your family thrive with books, DVDs, and more at **FocusOnTheFamily.com/resources**.

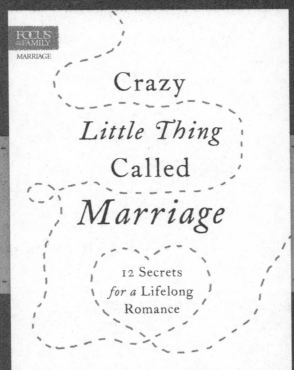